102 Lung Cancer Juice and Salad Recipes:

The Definitive Recipe Book to Treating and Preventing Cancer

By

Joe Correa CSN

COPYRIGHT

© 2019 Live Stronger Faster Inc.

All rights reserved

Reproduction or translation of any part of this work beyond that permitted by section 107 or 108 of the 1976 United States Copyright Act without the permission of the copyright owner is unlawful.

This publication is designed to provide accurate and authoritative information in regard to the subject matter covered. It is sold with the understanding that neither the author nor the publisher is engaged in rendering medical advice. If medical advice or assistance is needed, consult with a doctor. This book is considered a guide and should not be used in any way detrimental to your health. Consult with a physician before starting this nutritional plan to make sure it's right for you.

ACKNOWLEDGEMENTS

This book is dedicated to my friends and family that have had mild or serious illnesses so that you may find a solution and make the necessary changes in your life.

102 Lung Cancer Juice and Salad Recipes:

The Definitive Recipe Book to Treating and Preventing Cancer

By

Joe Correa CSN

CONTENTS

Copyright

Acknowledgements

About The Author

Introduction

Commitment

102 Lung Cancer Juice and Salad Recipes: The Definitive Recipe Book to Treating and Preventing Cancer

Additional Titles from This Author

ABOUT THE AUTHOR

After years of Research, I honestly believe in the positive effects that proper nutrition can have over the body and mind. My knowledge and experience has helped me live healthier throughout the years and which I have shared with family and friends. The more you know about eating and drinking healthier, the sooner you will want to change your life and eating habits.

Nutrition is a key part in the process of being healthy and living longer so get started today. The first step is the most important and the most significant.

INTRODUCTION

102 Lung Cancer Juice and Salad Recipes: The Definitive Recipe Book to Treating and Preventing Cancer

By Joe Correa CSN

When we talk about lung cancer, your best options are colorful fruits and vegetables. These foods are full of antioxidants, including vitamins A and C which are proven to help fight off this type of cancer. Fruits like berries and vegetables like tomatoes, winter squash, and bell peppers are particularly good and your juices should be based on them. These foods, when combined correctly, can be very delicious.

Food has a big impact on our body and our health. Almost all diseases are directly related to the foods we eat which is why it's crucial to choose carefully what we put at the table. It has the power to heal our bodies from within, which is especially important for people who have lung cancer or any type of cancer. Sometimes, we consume unnatural quantities of pharmaceuticals that may or may not be effective which can ultimately weaken our immune system and our entire body.

In this book, I will share with you some valuable recipes

that will give your body the nutrients it needs in order to function properly and fight off all types of diseases. Implementing these recipes into your everyday life will have a powerful effect on your overall health. I honestly believe we have no choice but to forge our own path to wellness through adequate food choices. This primarily refers to fresh fruits and vegetables which are the key to good health. The more we are able to return to eating as nature intended, the better our chances will be of living a cancer-free life.

Having this in mind, I have created a wonderful collection of lung cancer preventing recipes that are tasty and effective. Enjoy them all!

COMMITMENT

In order to improve my condition, I *(your name)*, commit to eating more of these foods on a daily basis and to exercise at least 30 minutes daily:

- Berries (especially blueberries), peaches, cherries, apples, apricots, oranges, lemon juice, grapefruit, tangerines, mandarins, pears, etc.
- Broccoli, spinach, collard greens, sweet potatoes, avocado, artichoke, baby corn, carrots, celery, cauliflower, onions, etc.
- Whole grains, steel-cut oats, oatmeal, quinoa, barley, etc.
- Black beans, red bean beans, garbanzo beans, lentils, etc.
- Nuts and seeds including: walnuts, cashews, flaxseeds, sesame seeds, etc.
- Fish
- 8 – 10 glasses of water

Sign here

X_____

102 LUNG CANCER JUICE AND SALAD RECIPES: THE DEFINITIVE RECIPE BOOK TO TREATING AND PREVENTING CANCER

1. Spinach Broccoli Juice

Ingredients:

1 cup of fresh spinach, torn

1 cup of broccoli, chopped

1 small Granny Smith's apple, cored

1 cup of green grapes

1 tbsp fresh mint, finely chopped

Preparation:

Using a large colander, rinse the spinach and broccoli under cold running water. Slightly drain and torn the spinach in small pieces. Trim off the outer leaves of the broccoli and cut into small pieces. Fill the measuring cups and set aside.

Wash the apple and cut lengthwise in half. Remove the core and cut into bite-sized pieces. Set aside.

Wash the grapes and remove the stem. Set aside.

Now, combine spinach, broccoli, apple, and grapes in a juicer and process until well juiced. Transfer to a serving glass and sprinkle with some fresh mint.

Refrigerate for 10 minutes before serving.

Nutrition information per serving: Kcal: 176, Protein: 9.8g, Carbs: 49.5g, Fats: 1.7g

2. Blueberry Beet Juice

Ingredients:

1 cup of blueberries

1 whole lime, peeled

1 large banana, sliced

1 cup of Romaine lettuce, shredded

1 whole cucumber, sliced

Preparation:

Rinse the blueberries using a small colander. Slightly drain and fill the measuring cup. Set aside.

Peel the lime and cut lengthwise in half. Set aside.

Peel the banana and cut into thin slices. Set aside.

Rinse the lettuce thoroughly under cold running water. Shred it and fill the measuring cup. Set aside.

Wash the cucumber and cut into thin slices. Set aside.

Now, combine blueberries, lime, banana, lettuce, and cucumber in a juicer and process until juiced. Transfer to a serving glass and add some crushed ice.

Serve immediately.

Nutrition information per serving: Kcal: 176, Protein: 9.8g, Carbs: 49.5g, Fats: 1.7g

3. Avocado Beet Juice

Ingredients:

1 cup of avocado, chopped

1 cup of beets, trimmed

1 large carrot, sliced

1 small ginger knob

¼ tsp turmeric, ground

2 oz water

Preparation:

Peel the avocado and cut lengthwise in half. Remove the pit and cut into bite-sized pieces. Fill the measuring cup and reserve the rest in the refrigerator.

Trim off the green parts of the beets. Slightly peel and cut into thin slices. Fill the measuring cup and refrigerate the rest.

Wash and peel the carrot. Cut into bite-sized pieces and set aside.

Peel the ginger knob and cut into small pieces. Set aside.

Now, combine avocado, beets, carrot, and ginger in a

juicer. Process until well juiced and transfer to a serving glass. Stir in the turmeric and water and refrigerate for 15 minutes before serving.

Enjoy!

Nutrition information per serving: Kcal: 265, Protein: 5.9g, Carbs: 33.4g, Fats: 21.8g

4. Pomegranate Cantaloupe Juice

Ingredients:

1 cup of pomegranate seeds

1 large wedge of cantaloupe

1 small green apple, cored

1 small ginger knob, sliced

1 oz of water

Preparation:

Cut the top of the pomegranate fruit using a sharp paring knife. Slice down to each of the white membranes inside of the fruit. Pop the seeds into a measuring cup and set aside.

Cut the cantaloupe in half. Scrape out the seeds and cut one one large wedge. Peel and chop into small pieces. Wrap the rest in a plastic foil and refrigerate for later.

Wash the apple and cut lengthwise in half. Remove the core and cut into bite-sized pieces. Set aside.

Peel the ginger and cut into small pieces. Set aside.

Now, combine pomegranate, cantaloupe, apple, and ginger in a juicer. Process until well juiced and transfer to a serving glass. Add some water to adjust the bitterness, if needed.

Refrigerate for 10-15 minutes before serving.

Nutrition information per serving: Kcal: 162, Protein: 3.1g, Carbs: 45.3g, Fats: 1.5g

5. Grapefruit Apricot Juice

Ingredients:

2 whole grapefruits

1 cup of collard greens, chopped

2 whole apricots, pitted

¼ tsp of turmeric, ground

Preparation:

Peel the grapefruits and divide into wedges. Cut each wedge in half and set aside.

Wash the collard greens thoroughly under cold running water. Drain and chop into small pieces. Set aside.

Wash the apricots and cut lengthwise in half. Remove the pit and cut into bite-sized pieces. Set aside.

Now, combine grapefruit, collard greens, and apricots in a juicer and process until juiced. Transfer to a serving glass and stir in the turmeric.

Refrigerate for 10 minutes before serving.

Nutrition information per serving: Kcal: 208, Protein: 5.8g, Carbs: 62.1g, Fats: 1.2g

6. Honeydew Melon Cucumber Juice

Ingredients:

1 large wedge of honeydew melon

1 cup of cucumber, sliced

1 cup of whole cranberries

2 large strawberries

1 oz coconut water

Preparation:

Cut melon lengthwise in half. Scoop out the seeds and then wash the melon. Cut one wedge and peel it. Cut into bite-sized pieces and set aside.

Wash the cucumber and cut into thin slices. Fill the measuring cup and reserve the rest for later. Set aside.

Using a small colander, rinse well the cranberries. Drain and set aside.

Wash the strawberries and remove the stems. Chop into small pieces and set aside.

Now, combine melon, cucumber, cranberries, and strawberries in a juicer. Process until well juiced. Transfer to a serving glass and add few ice cubes.

Serve immediately.

Nutrition information per serving: Kcal: 96, Protein: 1.8g, Carbs: 31.4g, Fats: 0.6g

7. Cauliflower Artichoke Juice

Ingredients:

1 cup of cauliflower, chopped

1 medium artichoke, chopped

1 whole lemon, peeled and halved

1 small zucchini, thinly sliced

1 small ginger knob, chopped

¼ tsp salt

Preparation:

Trim off the outer layer of the cauliflower. Cut into bite-sized pieces and wash it. Fill the measuring cup and sprinkle with some salt. Set aside.

Trim off the outer layers of the artichoke using a sharp paring knife. Cut into bite-sized pieces and set aside.

Peel the lemon and cut lengthwise in half. Set aside.

Wash the zucchini and thinly slice it. Set aside.

Peel the ginger knob and chop into small pieces. Set aside.

Now, combine cauliflower, artichoke, lemon, zucchini, and

ginger in a juicer. Process until well juiced.

Transfer to a serving glass and refrigerate for 15 minutes before serving.

Enjoy!

Nutrition information per serving: Kcal: 82, Protein: 8.4g, Carbs: 28.9g, Fats: 1.1g

8. Pineapple Banana Juice

Ingredients:

1 cup of pineapple chunks

1 large banana, sliced

1 cup of blackberries

1 whole lime, peeled

1 oz of water

Preparation:

Using a sharp paring knife, cut the top of the pineapple. Gently remove all hard skin and slice it into thin slices. Fill the measuring cup and reserve the rest for later. Peel the banana and cut into thin slices. Set aside. Place the blackberries in a small colander and wash under cold running water. Slightly drain and set aside. Peel the lime and cut lengthwise in half. Set aside.

Now, combine pineapple, banana, blackberries, and lime in a juicer. Process until well juiced. Transfer to a serving glass and add some ice before serving.

Nutrition information per serving: Kcal: 222, Protein: 4.5g, Carbs: 70.2g, Fats: 1.4g

9. Bell Pepper Tomato Juice

Ingredients:

1 large red bell pepper, chopped

1 medium whole tomato, chopped

1 cup of watercress, torn

1 rosemary sprig

1 oz of water

Preparation:

Wash the bell pepper and cut lengthwise in half. Remove the seeds and chop into small pieces. Set aside.

Wash the tomato and place in a small bowl. Chop into small pieces and make sure to reserve the tomato juice while cutting. Set aside.

Wash the watercress thoroughly under cold running water. Slightly drain and torn with hands into small pieces. Set aside.

Now, combine bell pepper, tomato, and watercress in a juicer and process until juiced. Transfer to a serving glass and stir in the water and reserved tomato juice. Sprinkle with rosemary and serve immediately.

Enjoy!

Nutrition information per serving: Kcal: 56, Protein: 3.5g, Carbs: 15.1g, Fats: 0.7g

10. Pumpkin Carrot Juice

Ingredients:

1 cup of pumpkin, cubed

1 large carrot, sliced

1 cup of cucumber, sliced

1 large orange, peeled and wedged

1 small ginger knob, chopped

Preparation:

Cut the top of a pumpkin. Cut lengthwise in half and then scrape out the seeds. Cut one large wedge and peel it. Cut into small cubes and fill the measuring cup. Reserve the rest in the refrigerator.

Wash and peel the carrot. Cut into thin slices and set aside.

Wash the cucumber and cut into thin slices. Fill the measuring cup and reserve the rest for later. Set aside.

Peel the orange and divide into wedges. Cut each wedge in half and set aside.

Peel the ginger knob and cut into small pieces. Set aside.

Now, combine pumpkin, carrot, cucumber, orange, and

ginger in a juicer. Process until well juiced. Transfer to a serving glass and add some ice.

Serve immediately.

Nutrition information per serving: Kcal: 130, Protein: 4.1g, Carbs: 39.1g, Fats: 0.6g

11. Spinach Radish Juice

Ingredients:

1 cup of fresh spinach, torn

2 large radishes, chopped

1 cup of cucumber, sliced

1 cup of arugula, torn

¼ tsp turmeric, ground

Preparation:

Wash the spinach thoroughly under cold running water. Slightly drain and torn with hands. Set aside.

Wash the radishes and trim off the green parts. Peel and cut into thin slices. Set aside.

Wash the cucumber and cut into thin slices. Set aside.

Wash the arugula and torn with hands. Set aside.

Now, combine spinach, radish, cucumber, and arugula in a juicer and process until juiced. Transfer to a serving glass and stir in the turmeric.

Refrigerate for 15 minutes before serving.

Nutrition information per serving: Kcal: 53, Protein: 9.4g, Carbs: 15.3g, Fats: 1.1g

12. Apple Plum Juice

Ingredients:

1 medium-sized Red Delicious apple, cored

1 whole plum, cored

1 large banana, peeled and chunked

¼ tsp of cinnamon, ground

2 oz of water

Preparation:

Wash the apple and cut lengthwise in half. Remove the core and cut into bite-sized pieces. Set aside.

Wash the plum and cut in half. Remove the pit and cut into bite-sized pieces. Set aside.

Peel the banana and cut into small chunks. Set aside.

Now, combine apple, plum, and banana in a juicer and process until well juiced. Transfer to a serving glass and stir in the water and cinnamon.

Add few ice cubes before serving and enjoy!

Nutrition information per serving: Kcal: 238, Protein: 2.5g, Carbs: 68.4g, Fats: 1.1g

13. Broccoli Beet Juice

Ingredients:

2 cups of broccoli, chopped

1 cup of beets, trimmed and chopped

1 cup of fresh parsley, torn

1 cup of celery, chopped

¼ tsp of turmeric, ground

¼ tsp ginger, ground

Preparation:

Wash the broccoli and trim off the outer layers. Chop into small pieces and set aside.

Wash and peel the beets. Trim off the green ends and chop into bite-sized pieces. Fill the measuring cup and reserve the rest for later.

Rinse the parsley under cold running water and slightly drain. Torn with hands into small pieces and set aside.

Wash the celery stalks and chop it into bite-sized pieces. Fill the measuring cup and set aside.

Now, combine broccoli, beets, parsley, and celery in a

juicer and process until juiced. Transfer to a serving glass and stir in the turmeric and ginger.

Refrigerate for 10 minutes before serving.

Nutrition information per serving: Kcal: 109, Protein: 9.8g, Carbs: 31.8g, Fats: 1.5g

14. Watermelon Peach Juice

Ingredients:

1 cup of watermelon, cubed

1 large peach, pitted and chopped

1 medium-sized green apple, cored and chopped

1 small banana, chunked

¼ tsp of cinnamon, ground

Preparation:

Cut the watermelon in half. Cut one large wedge and wrap the rest in a plastic foil and refrigerate. Peel the slice and cut into small cubes. Remove the pits and fill the measuring cup. Set aside. Wash the peach and cut lengthwise in half. Remove the pit and chop into bite-sized pieces. Set aside. Peel the banana and cut into small chunks. Set aside.

Now, combine watermelon, peach, apple, and banana in a juicer and process until juiced. Transfer to a serving glass and stir in the cinnamon. Add some ice and serve immediately!

Nutrition information per serving: Kcal: 260, Protein: 4.4g, Carbs: 73.9g, Fats: 1.3g

15. Yellow Pepper Zucchini Juice

Ingredients:

1 large yellow bell pepper, chopped

1 medium-sized zucchini, sliced

1 cup of fresh basil, chopped

1 large carrot, sliced

¼ tsp of ginger, ground

Preparation:

Wash the bell pepper and cut lengthwise in half. Remove the stem and seeds. Cut into small pieces and set aside. Wash the zucchini and cut into small chunks. Set aside. Wash the basil thoroughly under cold running water. Slightly drain and chop into small pieces. Set aside. Wash and peel the carrot. Cut into thin slices and set aside. Now, combine pepper, zucchini, basil, and carrot in a juicer and process until juiced. Transfer to a serving glass and stir in the ginger. Add some water if needed. Refrigerate for 10 minutes before serving.

Nutrition information per serving: Kcal: 94, Protein: 5.6g, Carbs: 25.4g, Fats: 1.3g

16. Strawberry Spinach Juice

Ingredients:

1 cup of strawberries, chopped

1 cup of spinach, torn

1 whole lemon, peeled

1 whole lime, peeled

1 tbsp honey, raw

2 oz of water

Preparation:

Wash the strawberries and remove the stems. Cut into bite-sized pieces and set aside.

Wash the spinach thoroughly under cold running water. Slightly drain and torn into small pieces. Set aside.

Peel the lemon and lime. Cut each fruit lengthwise in half and set aside.

Now, combine strawberries, spinach, lemon, and lime in a juicer and process until juiced. Transfer to a serving glass and stir in the water and honey.

Garnish with some mint, but it's optional.

Refrigerate for 15 minutes before serving.

Enjoy!

Nutrition information per serving: Kcal: 81, Protein: 5.8g, Carbs: 27.8g, Fats: 1.4g

17. Asparagus Cauliflower Juice

Ingredients:

1 cup of asparagus, chopped

1 cup of cauliflower, chopped

1 cup of celery, chopped

1 cup of cucumber, sliced

¼ tsp of turmeric, ground

¼ tsp of cayenne pepper, ground

Preparation:

Wash the asparagus under cold running water. Trim off the woody ends and chop into bite-sized pieces. Set aside.

Wash the cauliflower and trim off the outer leaves. Chop into small pieces and fill the measuring cup. Reserve the rest for later.

Wash the celery and chop into bite-sized pieces. Set aside.

Wash the cucumber and cut into thin slices. Fill the measuring cup and reserve the rest in the refrigerator.

Now, combine asparagus, cauliflower, celery, and cucumber in a juicer and process until juiced. Transfer to a serving glass and stir in the turmeric and cayenne pepper.

Serve immediately.

Nutrition information per serving: Kcal: 52, Protein: 6.1g, Carbs: 15.4g, Fats: 0.7g

18. Cherry Lemon Juice

Ingredients:

1 cup of fresh cherries, pitted

1 whole lemon, peeled

1 medium-sized artichoke, chopped

1 medium-sized apple, cored

¼ tsp of cinnamon, ground

Preparation:

Wash the cherries using a large colander. Cut each in half and remove the pits. Set aside. Peel the lemon and cut lengthwise in half. Set aside. Wash the artichoke and trim off the outer, hard leaves. Cut into bite-sized pieces and set aside. Wash the apple and cut lengthwise in half. Remove the core and cut into bite-sized pieces. Set aside. Now, combine cherries, lemon, artichoke, and apple in a juicer and process until juiced. Transfer to a serving glass and stir in the cinnamon.

Refrigerate for 10 minutes before serving.

Nutrition information per serving: Kcal: 205, Protein: 7.2g, Carbs: 66.2g, Fats: 0.9g

19. Mango Blackberry Juice

Ingredients:

1 cup of mango, chopped

1 cup of blackberries

1 large banana, chunked

1 large orange, peeled

¼ tsp of cinnamon, ground

Preparation:

Wash the mango and cut into small chunks. Fill the measuring cup and reserve the rest for later.

Place the blackberries in a colander and wash under cold running water. Slightly drain and set aside.

Peel the banana and cut into small chunks. Set aside.

Peel the orange and divide into wedges. Cut each wedge in half and set aside.

Now, combine mango, blackberries, banana, and orange in a juicer and process until juiced. Transfer to a serving glass and stir in the cinnamon.

Add few ice cubes and serve immediately.

Nutrition information per serving: Kcal: 296, Protein: 6.6g, Carbs: 91.2g, Fats: 2.1g

20.   Avocado Carrot Juice

Ingredients:

1 cup of avocado, chunked

1 large carrot, chopped

1 cup of collard greens, torn

1 cup of Romaine lettuce, shredded

1 whole cucumber, sliced

¼ tsp of ginger, ground

Preparation:

Peel the avocado and cut lengthwise in half. Remove the pit and cut into small chunks. Fill the measuring cup and reserve the rest in the refrigerator.

Wash and peel the carrot. Cut into thin slices and set aside.

Combine collard greens and lettuce in a large colander. Wash thoroughly under cold running water. Drain and shred. Set aside.

Wash the cucumber and cut into thin slices. Fill the measuring cup and reserve the rest for later. Set aside.

Now, combine avocado, carrot, collard greens, lettuce, and

cucumber in a juicer and process until juiced. Transfer to a serving glass and stir in the ginger.

Refrigerate for 10 minutes before serving.

Nutrition information per serving: Kcal: 271, Protein: 7.3g, Carbs: 34.1g, Fats: 22.8g

21. Raspberry Pear Juice

Ingredients:

1 cup of raspberries

1 large pear, cored

1 whole plum, pitted and chopped

1 medium-sized Granny Smith's apple, cored

¼ tsp of cinnamon, ground

1 oz of coconut water

Preparation:

Wash the raspberries using a small colander. Slightly drain and set aside.

Wash the pear and cut lengthwise in half. Remove the core and cut into small pieces. Set aside.

Wash the plum and cut in half. Remove the pit and set aside.

Wash the apple and cut in half. Remove the core and cut into bite-sized pieces. Set aside.

Now, combine raspberries, pear, plum, and apple in a juicer and process until well juiced. Transfer to a serving glass and stir in the cinnamon and coconut water. Add some crushed ice and serve immediately.

Enjoy!

Nutrition information per serving: Kcal: 239, Protein: 3.5g, Carbs: 79.9g, Fats: 1.6g

22. Guava Mango Juice

Ingredients:

1 whole guava, chopped

1 cup of mango, chunked

1 tbsp of liquid honey

1 whole lime, peeled

1 cup of cucumber, sliced

1 medium-sized Golden Delicious apple, cored

Preparation:

Peel the guava using a sharp paring knife. Cut into bite-sized pieces and set aside.

Wash and peel the mango. Cut into small chunks and set aside.

Peel the lime and cut lengthwise in half. Set aside.

Wash the cucumber and cut into thin slices. fill the measuring cup and reserve the rest in the refrigerator.

Wash the apple and cut lengthwise in half. Remove the core and cut into bite-sized pieces. Set aside.

Now, combine guava, mango, lime, cucumber, and apple in a juicer and process until well juiced. Transfer to a serving glass and stir in the honey. Add some crushed ice and serve immediately.

Nutrition information per serving: Kcal: 211, Protein: 3.7g, Carbs: 61.1g, Fats: 1.5g

23. Blueberry Spinach Juice

Ingredients:

1 cup of blueberries

1 cup of fresh spinach, chopped

1 whole lime, peeled

1 medium-sized orange

1 oz coconut water

Preparation:

Place the blueberries in a colander and wash under cold running water. Slightly drain and set aside.

Wash the spinach thoroughly and drain. Chop into small pieces and set aside.

Peel the lime and cut lengthwise in half. Set aside.

Peel the orange and divide into wedges. Cut each wedge in half and set aside.

Now, combine blueberries, spinach, lime, and orange in a juicer and process until well juiced. Transfer to a serving glass and stir in the coconut water.

Sprinkle with some fresh mint. However, it's optional.

Enjoy!

Nutrition information per serving: Kcal: 158, Protein: 8.5g, Carbs: 48.1g, Fats: 1.5g

24. Pepper Broccoli Juice

Ingredients:

1 large green bell pepper, chopped

1 cup of broccoli, chopped

1 cup of Brussels sprouts, halved

1 whole lime, peeled

2 large carrots, sliced

¼ tsp turmeric, ground

Preparation:

Wash the bell pepper and cut lengthwise in half. Remove the stem and seeds. Chop into small pieces and set aside.

Wash the broccoli and Brussels sprouts. Trim off the wilted and outer leaves. Place in a heavy-bottomed pot and add water enough to cover all. Bring it to a boil and then remove from the heat. Drain well and chop into small pieces. Set aside to cool completely.

Peel the lime and cut lengthwise in half. Set aside.

Wash and peel the carrots. Cut into thin slices and set aside.

Now, combine bell pepper, broccoli, Brussels sprouts, lime, and carrots in a juicer and process until juiced. Transfer to a serving glasses and stir in the turmeric. Add some water, if needed.

Sprinkle with some salt, but it's optional.

Nutrition information per serving: Kcal: 122, Protein: 8.5g, Carbs: 39.1g, Fats: 1.2g

25. Cantaloupe Grapefruit Juice

Ingredients:

1 cup of cantaloupe, cubed

1 whole grapefruit

1 cup of fresh mint, torn

¼ tsp of cinnamon, ground

1 oz coconut water

Preparation:

Cut the cantaloupe in half. Scoop out the seeds and flesh. Cut and peel one large wedge. Chop into chunks and fill the measuring cup. Reserve the rest of the cantaloupe in a refrigerator.

Peel the grapefruit and divide into wedges. Cut each wedge in half and set aside.

Wash the mint thoroughly and torn with hands into small pieces. Set aside.

Now, combine cantaloupe, grapefruit, and mint in a juicer. Process until well juiced.

Transfer to a serving glass and stir in the cinnamon and

coconut water. Add some ice and serve immediately.

Nutrition information per serving: Kcal: 144, Protein: 4.2g, Carbs: 42.6g, Fats: 0.9g

26. Pomegranate Apple Juice

Ingredients:

1 cup of pomegranate seeds

1 medium-sized Granny Smith's apple, cored

1 large banana, chunked

1 tbsp of liquid honey

1 oz of water

Preparation:

Cut the top of the pomegranate fruit using a sharp paring knife. Slice down to each of the white membranes inside of the fruit. Pop the seeds into a measuring cup and set aside.

Wash the apple and cut lengthwise in half. Remove the core and cut into bite-sized pieces. Set aside.

Peel the banana and cut into small chunks. Set aside.

Now, combine pomegranate, apple, and banana in a juicer and process until juiced. Transfer to a serving glass and stir in the honey and water.

Serve cold.

Nutrition information per serving: Kcal: 243, Protein: 3.6g, Carbs: 70.1g, Fats: 1.8g

27. Zucchini Basil Juice

Ingredients:

1 medium-sized zucchini, chopped

1 cup of fresh basil, torn

1 cup of cucumber, sliced

1 cup of red leaf lettuce, torn

1 cup of avocado, cut into bite-sized pieces

Preparation:

Peel the zucchini and chop into small pieces. Set aside.

Combine basil and lettuce in a large colander and rinse under cold running water. Drain and torn with hands into small pieces. Set aside.

Peel the avocado and cut lengthwise in half. Remove the pit and cut into bite-sized pieces. Fill the measuring cup and reserve the rest in the refrigerator.

Wash the cucumber and cut into thin slices. Fill the measuring cup and refrigerate for later.

Now, combine zucchini, basil, lettuce, avocado, and cucumber in a juicer. Process until well juiced. Transfer to a serving glass and add some ice.

Serve immediately.

Nutrition information per serving: Kcal: 234, Protein: 6.7g, Carbs: 21.7g, Fats: 22.3g

28. Banana Peach Juice

Ingredients:

1 cup of banana, sliced

1 large peach, pitted and chopped

1 small green apple, cored and chopped

¼ tsp of cinnamon, ground

1 oz of coconut water

1 tbsp of mint, finely chopped

Preparation:

Peel the bananas and cut into thin slices. Fill the measuring cup and reserve the rest in the refrigerator.

Wash the peach and cut lengthwise in half. Remove the pit and cut into bite-sized pieces. Set side.

Wash the apple and cut in half. Remove the core and chop into small pieces. Set aside.

Now, combine bananas, peach, and apple in a juicer and process until well juiced. Transfer to a serving glass and stir in the cinnamon and coconut water. Add some crushed ice and sprinkle with finely chopped mint for some extra taste.

Enjoy!

Nutrition information per serving: Kcal: 362, Protein: 5.5g, Carbs: 104g, Fats: 1.7g

29. Swiss Chard-Tomato Juice

Ingredients:

1 cup of cherry tomatoes, halved

1 cup of Swiss chard, torn

1 cup of basil, torn

1 cup of beets, trimmed

¼ tsp of balsamic vinegar

¼ tsp of salt

1 oz of water

Preparation:

Wash the cherry tomatoes and remove the green stems. Cut in half and fill the measuring cup. Reserve the rest in the refrigerator for some other juice.

Combine Swiss chard and basil in a large colander and rinse thoroughly under cold running water. Drain and torn with hands into small pieces. Set aside.

Wash the beets and trim off the green parts. Cut into thin slices and fill the measuring cup. Reserve the rest for later.

Now, combine cherry tomatoes, Swiss chard, basil, and

beets in a juicer and process until juiced. Transfer to a serving glass and stir in the vinegar, salt, and water.

Serve immediately.

Nutrition information per serving: Kcal: 72, Protein: 5.1g, Carbs: 21.6g, Fats: 0.7g

30. Pear Apricot Juice

Ingredients:

1 large pear, chopped

3 whole apricots, pitted

1 cup of pomegranate seeds

1 medium-sized orange, wedged

¼ tsp of cinnamon, ground

Preparation:

Wash the pear and cut lengthwise in half. Cut into bite-sized pieces and set aside.

Wash the apricots and cut each in half. Remove the pit and cut into small pieces. Set aside.

Cut the top of the pomegranate fruit using a sharp paring knife. Slice down to each of the white membranes inside of the fruit. Pop the seeds into a measuring cup and set aside.

Peel the orange and divide into wedges. Cut each wedge in half and set aside.

Now, combine pear, apricots, pomegranate seeds, and orange in a juicer. Process until well juiced. Transfer to a serving glass and stir in the cinnamon.

Refrigerate for 10 minutes before serving.

Nutrition information per serving: Kcal: 253, Protein: 4.9g, Carbs: 78.3g, Fats: 1.9g

31. Kale Zucchini Juice

Ingredients:

1 cup of fresh kale, chopped

1 medium-sized zucchini, chopped

1 whole lemon, peeled

1 whole lime, peeled

1 cup of fresh mint, torn

Preparation:

Rinse the kale thoroughly under cold running water. Drain and chop into small pieces. Set aside.

Wash the zucchini and cut into small pieces. Set aside.

Peel the lemon and lime. Cut lengthwise in half and set aside.

Wash the mint and chop into small pieces. Set aside.

Now, combine kale, zucchini, lemon, lime, and mint in a juicer. Process until well juiced. Transfer to a serving glass and add some crushed ice.

Serve immediately.

Nutrition information per serving: Kcal: 79, Protein: 7g, Carbs: 24.7g, Fats: 1.7g

32. Kiwi Apricot Juice

Ingredients:

2 whole kiwis, peeled and halved

3 whole apricots, chopped

1 large green apple, cored

1 large banana, chunked

Preparation:

Peel the kiwi and cut lengthwise in half. Set aside.

Wash the apricots and cut in half. Remove the pits and cut into small pieces. Set aside.

Wash the apple and cut lengthwise in half. Remove the core and cut into bite-sized pieces. Set aside.

Peel the banana and cut into small chunks. Set aside.

Now, combine kiwi, apricots, apple, and banana in a juicer and process until juiced. Transfer to a serving glass and add some ice.

Serve immediately.

Nutrition information per serving: Kcal: 313, Protein: 5.4g, Carbs: 91g, Fats: 1.9g

33. Mango Mint Juice

Ingredients:

1 cup of mango, chunked

1 cup of fresh mint, torn

1 small Red Delicious apple, cored

1 medium-sized peach, pitted

Preparation:

Peel the mango and cut into small chunks. Fill the measuring cup and reserve the rest in the refrigerator.

Wash the mint thoroughly under cold running water and torn with hands. Set aside. You can soak mint in hot water for 2 minutes, but it's optional. Wash the apple and cut lengthwise in half. Remove the core and cut into bite-sized pieces. Set aside. Wash the peach and cut in half. Remove the pit and cut into small pieces. Set aside. Now, combine mango, mint, apple, and peach in a juicer and process until well juiced. Transfer to a serving glass and add few ice cubes.

Nutrition information per serving: Kcal: 227, Protein: 4.1g, Carbs: 64.9g, Fats: 1.6g

34. Orange Fennel Juice

Ingredients:

1 medium-sized orange, peeled

1 medium-sized pear, chopped

1 cup of fennel, chopped

1 whole lemon, peeled

¼ tsp of cinnamon, ground

1 oz of coconut water

Preparation:

Peel the orange and divide into wedges. Cut each wedge in half and set aside.

Wash the pear and cut in half. Remove the core and cut into small pieces. Set aside.

Trim off the outer wilted layers of the fennel. Roughly chop it and fill the measuring cup. Reserve the rest for later.

Peel the lemon and cut lengthwise in half. Set aside.

Now, combine orange, pear, fennel, and lemon in a juicer and process until well juiced. Transfer to a serving glass and stir in the cinnamon and coconut water.

Refrigerate for 15 minutes before serving.

Enjoy!

Nutrition information per serving: Kcal: 156, Protein: 3.6g, Carbs: 54.2g, Fats: 0.7g

35. Beet Raspberry Juice

Ingredients:

1 cup of beets, sliced

1 cup of raspberries

1 whole lemon, peeled

1 medium-sized pear, chopped

1 oz of water

Preparation:

Wash the beets and trim off the green parts. Cut into thin slices and fill the measuring cup. Reserve the rest for later.

Rinse well the raspberries using a small colander. Drain and set aside. Peel the lemon and cut lengthwise in half. Set aside. Wash the pear and cut in half. Remove the core and cut into bite-sized pieces. Set aside. Now, combine beets, raspberries, lemon, and pear in a juicer and process until juiced. Transfer to a serving glass and stir in the water.

Refrigerate for 10 minutes before serving.

Nutrition information per serving: Kcal: 165, Protein: 4.9g, Carbs: 60.2g, Fats: 1.4g

36. Sweet Potato Celery Juice

Ingredients:

1 cup of sweet potatoes, cubed

1 cup of celery, chopped

1 medium-sized apple, cored

1 medium-sized orange, peeled

1 tbsp of fresh mint, torn

Preparation:

Peel the sweet potato and cut into small cubes. Fill the measuring cup and reserve the rest for later. Set aside. Wash the celery and cut into bite-sized pieces. Set aside.

Wash the apple and cut lengthwise in half. Remove the core and cut into bite-sized pieces. Set aside. Peel the orange and divide into wedges. Cut each wedge in half and set aside. Now, combine sweet potatoes, celery, apple, and orange in a juicer. Process until well juiced. Transfer to a serving glass and sprinkle with mint. Add some crushed ice and serve immediately.

Nutrition information per serving: Kcal: 236, Protein: 4.7g, Carbs: 67.8g, Fats: 0.7g

37. Tomato Spinach Juice

Ingredients:

1 medium whole tomato, chopped

1 cup of fresh spinach, torn

1 medium-sized carrot, sliced

1 cup of celery, chopped

¼ tsp of salt

¼ tsp of balsamic vinegar

Preparation:

Wash the tomato and place in a small bowl. Cut into bite-sized pieces. Make sure to reserve the tomato juice while cutting. Set aside.

Wash the spinach thoroughly under cold running water. Torn into small pieces and set aside.

Wash and peel the carrot. Cut into thin slices and set aside.

Wash the celery and chop into small pieces. Set aside.

Now, combine tomato, spinach, carrot, and celery in a juicer and process until juiced. Transfer to a serving glass and stir in the salt, vinegar, and reserved tomato juice.

Serve cold.

Nutrition information per serving: Kcal: 72, Protein: 8.4g, Carbs: 21.2g, Fats: 1.4g

38. Strawberry Lime Juice

Ingredients:

1 cup of strawberries, chopped

1 whole lime, peeled

1 small Granny Smith's apple, cored

1 whole lemon, peeled

2 oz coconut water

¼ tsp cinnamon, ground

Preparation:

Wash the strawberries and remove the stems. Cut into bite-sized pieces and fill the measuring cup. Reserve the rest for later. Peel the lime and lemon. Cut each fruit in half and set aside. Wash the apple and cut lengthwise in half. Remove the core and cut into small pieces. Set aside. Now, combine strawberries, lime, lemon, and apple in a juicer and process until juiced. Transfer to a serving glass and stir in the coconut water and cinnamon. Add some crushed ice and serve immediately.

Nutrition information per serving: Kcal: 122, Protein: 2.4g, Carbs: 39.7g, Fats: 0.9g

39. Pineapple Orange Juice

Ingredients:

1 cup of pineapple, chunked

1 large orange, peeled

½ cup of spinach, torn

3 Brussels sprouts, halved

Preparation:

Using a sharp paring knife, cut the top of the pineapple. Gently remove all hard skin and slice it into thin slices. Fill the measuring cup and reserve the rest for later. Peel the orange and divide into wedges. Cut each wedge in half and set aside. Wash the spinach thoroughly under cold running water and torn with hands. Set aside. Wash the Brussels sprouts and trim off the wilted leaves. Cut each in half and set aside. Now, combine pineapple, orange, spinach, and Brussels sprouts in a juicer and process until well juiced. Transfer to a serving glass and refrigerate for 15 minutes before serving.

Nutrition information per serving: Kcal: 172, Protein: 7.9g, Carbs: 52.7g, Fats: 1.1g

40. Carrot Celery Juice

Ingredients:

1 large carrot, sliced

1 cup of celery, chopped

1 whole lemon, peeled

1 small Golden Delicious apple, cored

¼ tsp turmeric, ground

¼ tsp ginger, ground

Preparation:

Wash and peel the carrot. Cut into small slices and set aside. Wash the celery and cut into small pieces. Set aside. Peel the lemon and cut lengthwise in half. Set aside. Wash the apple and cut in half. Remove the core and cut into bite-sized pieces. Set aside. Now, combine carrot, celery, lemon, and apple in a juicer and process until juiced. Transfer to a serving glass and stir in the water, turmeric, and ginger. If you like, add some crushed ice.

Nutrition information per serving: Kcal: 105, Protein: 2.4g, Carbs: 32.8g, Fats: 0.7g

41. Pear Cabbage Juice

Ingredients:

1 large pear, chopped

1 cup of purple cabbage, chopped

1 whole lemon, peeled

1 whole cucumber, sliced

Preparation:

Wash the pear and cut lengthwise in half. Remove the core and chop into small pieces. Set aside.

Wash the cabbage thoroughly under cold running water. Drain and chop into small pieces. Set aside.

Peel the lemon and cut lengthwise in half. Set aside.

Wash the cucumber and cut into thin slices. Set aside.

Now, combine pear, cabbage, lemon, and cucumber in a juicer. Process until well juiced. Transfer to a serving glass and serve immediately.

Enjoy!

Nutrition information per serving: Kcal: 173, Protein: 4.7g, Carbs: 57.9g, Fats: 0.9g

42. Cauliflower Tomato Juice

Ingredients:

1 cup of cauliflower, chopped

1 medium-sized tomato, chopped

½ cup of spring onions, chopped

½ cup of basil, torn

1 cup of cucumber, sliced

1 oz of water

Preparation:

Trim off the outer leaves of the cauliflower. Wash it and cut into small pieces. Fill the measuring cup and reserve the rest for later. Set aside.

Wash the tomato and place in a small bowl. Chop into small pieces and reserve the tomato juice while cutting. Set aside.

Wash the spring onions and basil. Chop into small pieces. Set aside.

Wash the cucumber and cut into thin slices. Fill the measuring cup and reserve the rest for later. Set aside.

Now, combine cauliflower, tomato, spring onions, basil, and cucumber in a juicer and process until well juiced. Transfer to a serving glass and stir in the water.

Serve cold.

Nutrition information per serving: Kcal: 51, Protein: 4.4g, Carbs: 13.9g, Fats: 0.7g

43. Cantaloupe Strawberry Juice

Ingredients:

1 cup of cantaloupe, chopped

1 cup of strawberries, chopped

1 cup of banana, chunked

2 whole plums, chopped

¼ tsp of cinnamon, ground

Preparation:

Cut the cantaloupe in half. Scrape out the seeds and cut one one large wedge. Peel and chop into small pieces and fill the measuring cup. Wrap the rest in a plastic foil and refrigerate for later.

Wash the strawberries and remove the stems. Cut into bite-sized pieces and set aside.

Peel the banana and cut into chunks. Fill the measuring cup and reserve the rest. Set aside.

Wash the plums and cut each in half. Remove the pits and cut into small pieces. Set aside.

Now, combine cantaloupe, strawberries, banana, and

plums in a juicer and process until juiced. Transfer to a serving glass and stir in the cinnamon.

Add some crushed ice and serve immediately.

Nutrition information per serving: Kcal: 249, Protein: 4.8g, Carbs: 73.1g, Fats: 1.5g

44. Swiss Chard Kale Juice

Ingredients:

2 cups of Swiss chard, torn

1 cup of fresh kale, torn

1 cup of pomegranate seeds

1 large orange, peeled

1 small Granny Smith's apple, cored

Preparation:

Combine Swiss chard and kale in a large colander. Rinse under cold running water and drain. Torn into small pieces and set aside.

Cut the top of the pomegranate fruit using a sharp paring knife. Slice down to each of the white membranes inside of the fruit. Pop the seeds into a measuring cup and set aside.

Peel the orange and divide into wedges. Cut each wedge in half and set aside.

Wash the apple and cut lengthwise in half. Remove the core and cut into bite-sized pieces. Set aside.

Now, combine Swiss chard, kale, pomegranate seeds,

orange, and apple in a juicer and process until juiced. Transfer to a serving glass and add few ice cubes.

Serve immediately.

Nutrition information per serving: Kcal: 227, Protein: 7.9g, Carbs: 66.1g, Fats: 2.3g

45. Pineapple Mango Juice

Ingredients:

1 cup of pineapple, chunked

1 cup of mango, chopped

1 cup of kale, torn

1 large orange, peeled

1 small ginger knob, chopped

Preparation:

Using a sharp paring knife, cut the top of the pineapple. Gently remove all hard skin and cut it into small chunks. Fill the measuring cup and reserve the rest for later.

Peel the mango and chop into small pieces. Fill the measuring cup and reserve the rest for later. Set aside.

Wash the kale thoroughly under cold running water. Drain and torn into small pieces. Set aside.

Peel the orange and divide into wedges. Cut each wedge in half and set aside.

Peel the ginger knob and cut into small pieces. Set aside.

Now, combine pineapple, mango, kale, orange, and ginger

in a juicer and process until juiced. Transfer to a serving glass and refrigerate for 15 minutes before serving.

Enjoy!

Nutrition information per serving: Kcal: 258, Protein: 6.9g, Carbs: 74.9g, Fats: 1.7g

46. Pepper Cabbage Juice

Ingredients:

1 large red bell pepper, chopped

1 cup of purple cabbage, chopped

1 cup of beets, sliced

1 cup of fresh spinach, torn

3 cherry tomatoes, halved

¼ tsp of salt

Preparation:

Wash the bell pepper and cut lengthwise in half. Remove the stem and seeds. Cut into small pieces and set aside.

Combine cabbage and spinach in a large colander. Rinse thoroughly under cold running water and drain. Torn into small pieces and set aside.

Wash the beets and trim off the green parts. Peel and cut into thin slices and fill the measuring cup. Reserve the rest for later.

Wash the cherry tomatoes and remove the stems. Cut into halves and set aside.

Now, combine bell pepper, cabbage, beets, spinach, and tomatoes in a juicer and process until juiced. Transfer to a serving glass and stir in the salt.

Serve immediately.

Nutrition information per serving: Kcal: 134, Protein: 11.5g, Carbs: 39.1g, Fats: 1.8g

47. Blueberry Cucumber Juice

Ingredients:

1 cup of blueberries

1 cup of cucumber, sliced

1 cup of strawberries, chopped

1 cup of fresh mint, torn

1 large carrot, sliced

¼ tsp of cinnamon, ground

Preparation:

Wash the blueberries using a small colander. Drain and set aside.

Wash the cucumber and cut into thin slices. Fill the measuring cup and reserve the rest in the refrigerator.

Wash the strawberries and remove the stems. Chop into small pieces and set aside.

Wash the mint thoroughly under cold running water. Drain and torn into small pieces. Set aside.

Wash and peel the carrot. Cut into thin slices and set aside.

Now, combine blueberries, cucumber, strawberries, mint, and carrot in a juicer. Process until well juiced.

Transfer to a serving glass and stir in the cinnamon. Add some crushed ice and serve immediately!

Nutrition information per serving: Kcal: 141, Protein: 4g, Carbs: 45g, Fats: 1.3g

48. Grape Cherry Juice

Ingredients:

2 cups of green grapes

1 cup of frozen cherries, thawed

1 small banana, peeled

1 whole lime, peeled

1 tbsp of coconut water

Preparation:

Rinse the grapes under cold running water and remove the stems. Set aside.

Peel the banana and cut into chunks. Set aside.

Peel the lime and cut lengthwise in half. Set aside

Now, combine grapes, cherries, banana, and lime in a juicer and process until juiced. Transfer to a serving glass and stir in the coconut water.

Serve immediately.

Nutrition information per serving: Kcal: 292, Protein: 4.1g, Carbs: 82.9g, Fats: 1.3g

49. Lemon Leek Juice

Ingredients:

1 whole lemon, peeled

1 whole leek, chopped

1 whole lime, peeled

1 large orange, peeled

1 small green apple, cored

Preparation:

Peel the lemon and lime. Cut each fruit lengthwise in half and set aside. Wash the leek and chop into small pieces. Set aside. Peel the orange and divide into wedges. Cut each wedge in half and set aside. Wash the apple and cut in half. Remove the core and cut into small pieces. Set aside. Now, combine lemon, leek, lime, orange, and apple in a juicer and process until juiced. Transfer to a serving glass and refrigerate for 15 minutes before serving.

Enjoy!

Nutrition information per serving: Kcal: 205, Protein: 4.5g, Carbs: 62.9g, Fats: 0.9g

50. Avocado Radish Juice

Ingredients:

1 cup of avocado, cubed

3 large radishes, chopped

1 small zucchini, sliced

1 cup of celery, chopped

1 cup of cucumber, sliced

¼ tsp of salt

1 oz of water

Preparation:

Peel the avocado and cut in half. Remove the pit and cut into small cubes. Fill the measuring cup and reserve the rest for later.

Wash the radishes and cut into small pieces. Set aside.

Wash the zucchini and cut into thin slices. Set aside.

Wash the celery and chop it into bite-sized pieces. Set aside.

Wash the cucumber and cut into thin slices. Fill the

measuring cup and reserve the rest for later. Set aside.

Now, combine avocado, radishes, zucchini, celery, and cucumber in a juicer and process until juiced. Transfer to a serving glass and stir in the salt and water.

Serve cold.

Nutrition information per serving: Kcal: 235, Protein: 5.6g, Carbs: 22.3g, Fats: 22.6g

SALAD RECIPES

1. Sweet Potato and Walnut Salad

Ingredients:

1 medium sweet potato, cut into chunks

2 eggs, hard-boiled

7oz chicken breast, boneless and skinless

1 medium onion, diced

3 garlic cloves, crushed

1oz walnuts, finely chopped

2 tbsp olive oil

1 tbsp parsley, finely chopped

Salt and freshly ground black pepper to taste

Preparation:

Rinse potatoes thoroughly under cold running water. Pat dry and place on a clean work surface. Using a sharp knife, cut into bite-sized pieces and add to a deep, heavy-bottomed pan. Pour in enough water to cover and sprinkle with some salt.

Bring potatoes to a boil and cook until fork tender. When done, remove from the heat and drain. Set aside to cool.

Meanwhile, add eggs to a pot of boiling water and cook for 12 minutes. Remove from the heat and drain. Cool to a room temperature and then peel. Slice eggs and transfer to a serving bowl along with potatoes. Set aside.

Now, peel and chop onions. Add to a bowl along with crushed garlic. Sprinkle with one tablespoon of olive oil, parsley, salt, pepper, and walnuts. Mix all well and set aside.

Rinse the meat under cold running water and pat dry with a kitchen towel. Place ona a cutting board and chop into bite-sized pieces.

Grease a medium pan with the remaining oil and preheat over medium-high heat. Add the meat and sprinkle with some salt. Pour in about ¼ cup of water and cover with the lid. Cook, covered, for 15 minutes.

Remove the lid and continue to cook until all the liquid has evaporated. Cool for a while and serve over the prepared salad.

Nutritional information per serving: Kcal: 464, Protein: 32.1g, Carbs: 20.3g, Fats: 29.4g

2. Black Bean and Buckwheat Salad

Ingredients:

1 cup buckwheat groats

1 ripe avocado, sliced

1 small purple onion, diced

2 cups spinach, chopped

1 cup black beans, drained

1 cucumber

2 tbsp lime juice

2 tbsp olive oil

2 tbsp sesame seeds

1 tbsp honey

½ tsp cumin powder

1 small chili, diced

Salt and pepper to taste

Preparation:

Add buckwheat to a small pan and pour in 2 cups of water.

Bring to a boil and reduce the heat to medium. Gently simmer for 10-15 minutes or until buckwheat has absorbed all the liquid. Remove from the heat and set aside.

Meanwhile, prepare the vegetables. Rinse spinach under cold running water and drain in a large colander. Transfer to a bowl.

Peel and slice avocado, slice cucumber, and chop the onion. Transfer all to a serving bowl and add buckwheat and drained beans. Mix all well and set aside.

In a small bowl, whisk together lime juice, olive oil, sesame seeds, honey, cumin powder, diced chili, salt and pepper.

Pour the mixture over salad and stir well. Serve immediately.

Nutritional information per serving: Kcal: 410, Protein: 12.3g, Carbs: 50.2g, Fats: 20.9g

3. Tomato and Arugula Salad with Macadamia Nuts

Ingredients:

1 ripe tomato, cut into bite-sized pieces

2 small onions, diced

1 garlic clove, crushed

2 cups arugula, torn

2oz macadamia nuts, chopped

½ cup heavy cream

½ chicken stock cube

3 tbsp plain Greek yogurt

1 tsp lemon zest

Salt to taste

Preparation:

Wash tomato and slice into bite-sized pieces. Add to a bowl.

Peel and chop onions. Transfer to a medium sieve and generously sprinkle with salt. Let it sit for 10-12 minutes to remove the bitterness. Rinse thoroughly under cold running water and drain. Transfer to a bowl with tomato and add garlic and arugula. Set aside.

Add heavy cream to a small saucepan and gently heat up over medium heat. Add chicken stock cube, Greek yogurt, lemon zest, and some salt. Mix all well and cook for 2-3 minutes, stirring constantly.

Remove the mixture from the heat and cool to a room temperature.

Drizzle over salad and serve.

Nutritional information per serving: Kcal: 370, Protein: 7.6g, Carbs: 15.4g, Fats: 33.3g

4. Red Pepper Salad with Chicken and Pine Nuts

Ingredients:

7oz chicken breast, boneless and skinless

2 cups lettuce, chopped

1 red bell pepper, diced

½ cucumber, sliced

1oz pine nuts

3 tbsp plain Greek yogurt

2 tsp Worcestershire sauce

2 tbsp parsley, finely chopped

Salt

Preparation:

Preheat the oven to 400 degrees F. Line a small baking pan with some parchment paper and set aside.

Rinse the meat under cold running water and pat dry with a kitchen paper. Transfer to a cutting board and chop into bite-sized pieces. Set aside.

In a small bowl, mix together Greek yogurt, Worcestershire

sauce, parsley, and salt. Sprinkle the meat with this mixture and bake for 15 minutes.

Remove the meat from the oven and cool to a room temperature.

Meanwhile, wash and prepare vegetables. Rinse lettuce under cold running water and add to serving bowl.

Wash the bell pepper and remove the stem. Slice in half, lenghtwise and remove the seeds. Rinse well again and slice into bite-sized pieces. Add to a bowl along with sliced cucumber and pine nuts.

Top with the meat and mix all well. Serve.

Nutritional information per serving: Kcal: 269, Protein: 25.7g, Carbs: 13.6g, Fats: 12.8g

5. Artichoke Salad Toast

Ingredients:

7oz artichoke spears, chopped into bite-sized pieces

2 garlic cloves, crushed

1 small onion, diced

½ avocado, sliced

1 tbsp olive oil

1oz raisins

Salt and pepper to taste

4 slices whole wheat toast bread

Preparation:

Grease a small skillet with olive oil and heat over medium heat. Add onions and garlic and saute until translucent, stirring constantly.

Now, add artichoke spears and cook for 5 minutes. Remove from the heat and cool for a while.

Meanwhile, peel and finely chop onions. Add to a bowl along with avocado, garlic, and raisins. Sprinkle with salt and pepper and add chilled artichoke spears. Set aside.

Lightly toast the bread and and serve with the prepared artichoke mixture. Serve.

Nutritional information per serving: Kcal: 423, Protein: 13.4g, Carbs: 55.8g, Fats: 19.1g

6. Mexican Lentil Salad

Ingredients:

1 cup brown lentils, drained

¾ cup sweet corn, drained

½ cup black beans, drained

2 tbsp walnuts, finely chopped

1 celery stalk, sliced

1 medium onion, diced

1 cup cherry tomatoes, sliced

1 chili pepper, diced

2 tbsp parsley, finely chopped

1 tbsp olive oil

Salt

Preparation:

Rinse and drain lentils, corn, and black beans. Transfer to serving bowl and set aside.

Peel and finely chop onions. Add to a bowl.

Slice each cherry tomato in half, lenthgwise and add to a bowl along with the remaining ingredients. Mix all well and sprinkle with olive oil and salt.

Serve.

Nutritional information per serving: Kcal: 450, Protein: 21.8g, Carbs: 64.7g, Fats: 13.8g

7. Warm Kale Salad

Ingredients:

1 head kale, medium

1 pear, sliced

¼ cup dried cranberries

¼ avocado, sliced

¼ cup orange juice, freshly squeezed

1 garlic clove, crushed

2 tbsp extra virgin olive oil

1 tbsp yellow mustard

¼ tsp sea salt

¼ tsp black pepper

2 tbsp apple cider vinegar

¼ tbsp brown sugar

Preparation:

In a small bowl, whisk together orange juice, garlic clove, olive oil, mustard, salt, pepper, apple cider vinegar, and sugar. Mix well and set aside.

Rinse kale under cold running water and add to a deep pan. Pour in enough water to cover and bring to a boil. Cook for 5 minutes.

Remove from the heat and drain. Transfer to a bowl along with pear, cranberries, and avocado. Mix well and sprinkle with the prepared dressing.

Serve.

Nutritional information per serving: Kcal: 269, Protein: 2.7g, Carbs: 24g, Fats: 19.4g

8. Garlic Eggplant Salad

Ingredients:

1 large eggplant, chopped into bite-sized pieces

4 large garlic cloves, chopped

½ cup walnuts, finely chopped

2 tbsp olive oil

1 tbsp apple cider vinegar

¼ cup cottage cheese

½ tsp smoked paprika

¼ tsp rosemary

Salt and pepper

Preparation:

Peel eggplant and cut into bite-sized pieces. Add to a medium sieve and generously sprinkle with salt. Let it sit for 15 minutes.

After about 15 minutes, rinse eggplant thoroughly under cold running water and drain. Set aside.

Grease a medium pan with olive oil and heat up to

medium-high heat. Add garlic and cook for 1-2 minutes, stirring constantly.

Now, add drained eggplants and continue to cook for 15 minutes, stirring occasionally.

Meanwhile, in a small bowl, combine together apple cider vinegar, smoked paprika, rosemary, salt, and pepper.

Remove eggplants from the heat and trasnfer to a bowl. Add cottage cheese and walnuts. Sprinkle with apple cider mixture and stir well. Serve.

Nutritional information per serving: Kcal: 408, Protein: 14.1g, Carbs: 20.1g, Fats: 33.5g

9. Asparagus Salad with Dijon

Ingredients:

7oz asparagus, chopped into bite-sized pieces

1 small sweet potato, cut into chunks

1 tbsp dijon mustard

¼ cup plain Greek yogurt

1 tbsp parsley, finely chopped

½ tsp dried thyme

¼ tsp dried marjoram

2 tsp balsamic vinegar

1 tsp sugar

Salt and pepper to taste

Preparation:

Preheat a large grill pan over medium heat. Add asparagus and cook for 4-5 minutes, turning occasionally. Remove from the heat and cool for a while.

Meanwhile, rinse potato thoroughly under cold running water and rub the skin. Cut into bite-sized pieces and add to a deep pot. Pour in enough water to cover and bring to a boil. Cook until fork tender.

Remove potatoes from the heat and drain. Cool to a room temperature and transfer to a bowl along with asparagus.

In a small bowl, whisk togetehr dijon, Greek yogurt, parsley, thyme, marjoram, balsamic vinegar, sugar, salt, and pepper. Pour the mixture over salad and serve.

Nutritional information per serving: Kcal: 165, Protein: 12.2g, Carbs: 27.9g, Fats: 1.8g

10. Buckwheat and Lettuce Salad

Ingredients:

½ cup buckwheat groats

1 medium carrot, diced

1 cup lettuce, torn

2oz smoked salmon

2 tbsp olive oil

1 tbsp apple cider vinegar

Salt and pepper to taste

Preparation:

Add buckwheat to a small saucepan and pour in one cup of water. Sprinkle with some salt and bring to a boil over medium heat. Cook until buckwheat has absorbed all the liquid, about 12-15 minutes.

When done, remove from the heat and drain. Cool to a room temperature.

Transfer buckwheat to a bowl and add carrot, lettuce, and smoked salmon. Sprinkle with olive oil, apple cider vinegar, salt, and pepper.

Nutritional information per serving: Kcal: 543, Protein: 18.7g, Carbs: 50.1g, Fats: 32.4g

11. French Octopus Salad

Ingredients:

1 lb of fresh octopus

1 small onion, finely chopped

10 cherry tomatoes

¼ cup green olives

1 tbsp of capers

2 tbsp olive oil

2 tbsp freshly squeezed apple juice

1 tbsp of finely chopped parsley

Salt to taste

Preparation:

Place the octopus in a pressure cooker. Add 2 cups of water and seal the lid. Cook for about 40-45 minutes. Remove from the heat and allow it to cool for a while. Slice the octopus into bite-sized pieces and set aside.

Preheat two tablespoons of olive oil in a large skillet. Add the onions and stir-fry for five minutes. Now add apple juice, parsley, and octopus. Mix well and fry for about five more minutes. Remove from the heat and transfer to a bowl. Add halved cherry tomatoes, olives, and capers. Sprinkle with apple juice, parsley, and salt.

Keep it in the refrigerator for at least an hour before serving.

You can serve this salad with Swiss chard, or leeks.

Nutrition information per serving: Kcal: 328, Protein: 24.3g, Carbs: 11.3g, Fats: 21g

12. Orange Shrimp Salad

Ingredients:

1 lb large shrimps, peeled and deveined

2 tbsp freshly squeezed orange juice

1 tbsp cayenne pepper

1 tsp freshly ground black pepper

1 tsp pink Himalayan salt

4 garlic cloves, crushed

3 tbsp extra virgin olive oil

2 tablespoons fresh parsley, finely chopped

1 cup lettuce, chopped

1 large tomato, chopped

1 medium purple onion, diced

½ red bell pepper, sliced

Preparation:

In a large skillet, heat up the oil over medium-high heat. Add garlic and cook for 1 minute, stirring constantly. Now, throw in the shrimps and cook until nice golden color.

Remove from the heat and cool for a while.

Meanwhile, wash and prepare the vegetables. Chop each piece and add to a bowl along with shrimps.

In a small bowl, whisk together orange juice, cayenne pepper, salt, black pepper, and parsley. Drizzle over salad and serve.

Nutrition information per serving: Kcal: 391, Protein: 43.6g, Carbs: 10.1g, Fats: 21.6g

13. Mussel and Arugula Salad

Ingredients:

10oz fresh mussels, debearded

1 medium onion, peeled and finely chopped

2 garlic cloves, crushed

1 tbsp fresh lemon juice

¼ cup fresh parsley, finely chopped

1 tbsp rosemary, finely chopped

1 cup lamb's lettuce, chopped

1 cup arugula leaves, chopped

1 cup cherry tomatoes, sliced

Sea salt to taste

Preparation:

Rinse and drain the mussels. Set aside.

Grease a non-stick frying pan with some cooking spray and heat over medium heat. Add onions and garlic. Cook until translucent.

Now, add mussels and continue to cook until crisp-tender.

Season with salt, pepper, and rosemary. Remove from the heat and cool for a while.

Meanwhile, wash and prepare vegetables. Add to a bowl along with mussels and mix all well.

Stir in parsley and lemon juice. Season with some more salt and pepper to taste and serve immediately.

Nutrition information per serving: Kcal: 358, Protein: 38.4g, Carbs: 34.1g, Fats: 7.7g

14. Spring Salad with Olives

Ingredients:

2 cups cherry tomatoes, sliced

1 cup black olives

1 medium onion, diced

2 radishes, sliced

A handful of lamb's lettuce

2 tbsp of freshly squeezed lime juice

3 tbsp of extra virgin olive oil

2 tbsp plain Greek yogurt

2 tbsp almonds, chopped

1 tbsp sesame seeds

1 tsp apple cider vinegar

Salt to taste

Preparation:

In a small bowl, whisk together olive oil, lime juice, Greek yogurt, chopped almonds, sesame seeds, apple cider vinegar, and salt. Set aside.

Slice each cherry tomato in half and add to a bowl along with olives, diced onions and sliced radishes.

Rinse lamb's lettuce thoroughly under cold running water and drain in a large sieve. Transfer to a bowl and mix well.

Drizzle with the almond mixture and toss to combine. Serve.

Nutrition information per serving: Kcal: 329, Protein: 3.4g, Carbs: 20.1g, Fats: 28.7g

15. Fresh Tomato Salad

Ingredients:

5-6 cherry tomatoes

1 medium onion, chopped

A handful of fresh lettuce, torn

½ cup fresh celery leaves, chopped

½ tsp dried oregano

½ tsp pink Himalayan salt

1 tbsp freshly squeezed lemon juice

Preparation:

Peel and finely chop onion. Place in a medium sieve and sprinkle with some salt. Let it sit for 10-12 minutes to remove the bitterness.

When done, rinse well under cold running water and drain. Add to a bowl along with sliced cherry tomatoes.

Wash lettuce and chop with your hands. Add to a bowl and mix well. Sprinkle with salt, oregano, and lemon juice before serving.

Nutrition information per serving: Kcal: 169, Protein: 7.2g, Carbs: 36.5g, Fats: 1.6g

16. Spinach Salad with Leeks

Ingredients:

12oz fresh spinach

3 large leeks, sliced

2 red onions, sliced

2 garlic cloves, crushed

2 tbsp goat's cheese

3 tbsp extra virgin olive oil

1 tsp sea salt

Preparation:

Heat up the olive oil over medium-high heat. Add sliced leek, garlic, and onions. Stir-fry for about five minutes, over medium heat.

Now add spinach and give it a good stir. Season with sea salt and continue to cook for 3 more minutes, stirring constantly.

Remove from the heat and sprinkle with fresh goat's cheese for some extra taste. However, keep in mind that even goat's cheese is slightly acidic. You have to limit the intake to maximum one tablespoon per serving.

Serve immediately.

Nutrition information per serving: Kcal: 301, Protein: 9.6g, Carbs: 24.7g, Fats: 20.4g

17. Chickpea Salad with Onions

Ingredients:

1 lb chickpeas, soaked

3 large purple onions, peeled and sliced

2 large tomatoes, roughly chopped

3 tbsp parsley, chopped

2 cups vegetable broth

1 tbsp cayenne pepper

2 tbsp olive oil

1 tsp salt

½ tsp freshly ground black pepper

Preparation:

Preheat the oil in a large saucepan over a medium-high heat. Add onions and saute for 4-5 minutes, or until translucent.

Now, add chickpeas, tomatoes, parsley, and vegetable broth.

Stir in cayenne pepper, salt, and freshly ground black pepper. Cover with a lid and bring it to a boil. Reduce the heat to low and cook for 25 minutes. Remove from the heat and cool to a room temperature.

Transfer to the refrigerator for at least an hour before serving.

Nutrition information per serving: Kcal: 513, Protein: 21.8g, Carbs: 68.3g, Fats: 19.1g

18. Greek Salad with Fresh Goat's Cheese

Ingredients:

5oz fresh goat's cheese

1 egg, boiled

1 cup red cabbage, shredded

Few lettuce leaves

1 medium tomato, chopped

1 small onion, sliced

½ cucumber, sliced

½ red bell pepper, sliced

Few olives

1 chili pepper, diced

2 tbsp cup olive oil

1 tsp mustard

1 tbsp finely chopped parsley

1 garlic clove, crushed

Sea salt to taste

Black pepper to taste

Preparation:

Gently place egg in a small pot and pour enough water to cover. Bring it to a boil and cook for 7 minutes. Remove from the heat and rinse under cold running water. Cool completely and peel. Transfer to a serving plate.

Wash and drain the vegetables. Cut and set aside.

Combine the olive oil with mustard, finely chopped parsley, and one garlic clove. Season with some salt and pepper and mix well.

Place the vegetables on a serving plate. Drizzle with the olive oil dressing and serve immediately.

Nutrition information per serving: Kcal: 283, Protein: 13.9g, Carbs: 11.7g, Fats: 21.3g

19. Halloumi Eggplant Salad

Ingredients:

2 medium eggplants, sliced in half

5oz halloumi cheese, sliced

2 large tomatoes, chopped

1 small cucumber, sliced

¼ cup fresh mint, chopped

¼ tsp dried marjoram

Salt to taste

<u>For grilling:</u>

2 tbsp olive oil

3 tbsp lemon juice, freshly squeezer

1 tsp red wine vinegar

½ tsp dried thyme

1 tbsp toasted sesame seeds

¼ tsp garlic powder

¼ tsp cumin powder

For dressing:

4 tbsp olive oil

1 small onion, diced

1 chili pepper, diced

¼ cup olives, sliced in half

3 tbsp pistachios, whole

1 tbsp lemon juice

Salt and pepper to taste

Preparation:

Slice eggplants lengthwise into ¼ inch thick slices. Generously sprinkle with salt and let it sit for 10 minutes. Rinse well the salt and drain. Pat dry with a piece of kitchen paper and set aside.

Slice halloumi into ½ inch thick slices. Set aside.

In a small bowl, whisk together all the ingredients for the grill – olive oil, lemon juice, red wine vinegar, thyme, sesame seeds, garlic powder, and cumin powder.

Brush eggplant and cheese with this mixture and set aside.

Preheat a large non-stick grill pan over medium-high heat. Add eggplant and cheese and grill until lightly golden brown. Remove from the pan and transfer to serving plate.

Meanwhile, combine all dressing ingredients in a small bowl. Pour the mixture over grilled eggplant and cheese.

Serve immediately.

Nutrition information per serving: Kcal: 457, Protein: 13.2g, Carbs: 27.8g, Fats: 35.9g

20. Quinoa Salad with Pomegranate Seeds

Ingredients:

½ cup quinoa

¼ cup buckwheat groats

1 blood orange, peeled

1 avocado, sliced

½ cup pomegranate seeds

1 cup baby spinach

½ cup cherry tomatoes, sliced

1 tbsp hazelnuts, chopped

1 tbsp sesame oil

Salt to taste

Preparation:

Add quinoa to a heavy-bottomed pot and pour in 1 ½ cup of water or vegetable stock. Bring to a boil over medium heat and cover with the lid. Reduce the heat to low and simmer for 15 minutes, stirring occasioanlly.

Remove quinoa from the heat and cool for a while. Set

aside.

Meanwhile, place buckwheat in a small pot and pour in enough water to cover. Soak for 15-20 minutes. When done, transfer to a large sieve and drain.

Add cooked quinoa and soaked buckwheat groats to a bowl and mix well.

Now, rinse spinach under cold running water and add to a bowl along with the remaining vegetables. Add pomegranate seeds, hazelnuts, sliced avocado, and sesame oil. Sprinkle with some salt and serve.

Nutrition information per serving: Kcal: 378, Protein: 8.1g, Carbs: 44g, Fats: 20.8g

21. Creamy Rice Salad with Corn

Ingredients:

½ cup rice

1 tomato, chopped

¼ cup corn, drained

1 cup arugula, chopped

2oz feta, cubed

1 tbsp olive oil

Salt and pepper to taste

1 tbsp lemon juice

Preparation:

Add rice to a deep pot and pour in 1 ½ of water. Sprinkle with some salt and bring to a boil. Reduce the heat to medium-low and cook until all the water has evaporated. Stir occasionally.

Remove from the heat and cool for a while. Transfer to a bowl and add tomato, corn, arugula, and feta.

Sprinkle with olive oil, salt, pepper, lemon juice. Stir all well and serve.

Nutrition information per serving: Kcal: 328, Protein: 8.5g, Carbs: 43.4g, Fats: 13.7g

22. Sour Cabbage Salad

Ingredients:

2 cups cabbage, shredded

½ cup radishes, sliced

1 medium purple onion, diced

2 eggs, boiled

2 tbsp olive oil

2 tsp apple cider vinegar

1 tsp Italian seasoning

Preparation:

Add eggs to a pot of boiling water and sprinkle with salt. Cook for 10-12 minutes. When done remove from the heat and drain. Cool eggs completely and then gently peel.

Slice eggs and add to a bowl.

Meanwhile, sprinkle cabbage with salt and let it sit for 10 minutes. Rinse well and drain. Transfer to a bowll along with diced onion and sliced radishes.

Sprinkle with olive oil, apple cider vinegar, and Italian seasoning.

Toss well to combine and serve.

Nutrition information per serving: Kcal: 471, Protein: 14.5g, Carbs: 21.6g, Fats: 38.5g

23. Mediterranean Fusilli Salad

Ingredients:

2oz dry fussilli

10oz shrimp tails, peeled

1 cup cherry tomatoes, sliced

1 purple onion, diced

1 green chili pepper, diced

1 avocado, sliced

½ cup green olives, pits removed

½ cup fresh goat's cheese

1 tbsp olive oil

1 tsp apple cider vinegar

1 tsp Italian seasoning

Preparation:

Add fussilli to a deep pot and pour in enough water to cover. Sprinkle with some salt and bring to a boil. Mix well and cook pasta until al dente. Remove from the heat and drain. Transfer to a bowl and set aside.

Grease a large pan with olive oil and heat up over high heat. Add shrimp tails and sprinkle with Italian seasoning. Cook for 3-4 minutes, turning once. Remove from the heat and add to a bowl with pasta.

Now, wash and prepare vegetables. Add to a bowl along with sliced avocado, olives, and goat's cheese. Sprinkle with apple cider vinegar and Italian seasoning.

Mix all well and serve.

Nutrition information per serving: Kcal: 387, Protein: 24.4g, Carbs: 27g, Fats: 21.3g

24. Baked Potato Salad with Onions

Ingredients:

1lb baby potatoes, whole

2oz smoked salmon

2 tbsp olive oil

2 large purple onions, sliced

2 garlic cloves, crushed

1 tbsp yellow mustard

1 tsp dried rosemary

Salt and pepper to taste

Preparation:

Preheat the oven to 350 degrees F. Line a baking sheet with parchment paper and set aside.

Rinse potatoes under cold running water and rub with salt. Add to the prepared baking sheet and sprinkle with rosemary. Bake for 40-45 minutes.

When done, remove from the oven and cool for a while.

Meanwhile, whisk together olive oil, crushed garlic,

mustard, and some salt and pepper. Brush potatoes with this mixture and trasnfer to serving plate.

Add onions and smoked salmon. Serve.

Nutrition information per serving: Kcal: 356, Protein: 13.2g, Carbs: 44g, Fats: 16g

25. Couscous Salad

Ingredients:

1 cup couscous

2 medium tomatoes, sliced

1 cup lettuce, chopped

¼ cup fresh mint

1 medium onion, diced

1 tbsp almond butter

1 tbsp lemon juice

Salt and pepper to taste

1 tbsp olive oil

Preparation:

Add couscous to a deep, heavy-bottomed pot and pour in 1 ½ cup of water. Sprinkle with salt and bring to a boil. Reduce the heat to medium-low and cook for 10-15 minutes, or until couscous has absorbed all the liquid. Add almond butter and mix well. Remove from the heat and set aside.

Meanwhile, wash and prepare vegetables. Add to a bowl

along with couscous. Mix well.

Sprinkle with lemon juice, olive oil, salt, and pepper. Serve.

Nutrition information per serving: Kcal: 489, Protein: 15g, Carbs: 80.4g, Fats: 12.6g

26. Chili Bean Salad

Ingredients:

1 cup kidney beans, drained

1 green bell pepper, sliced

3 red chili peppers, diced

2 tbsp pine nuts

1 tbsp macadamia nuts, chopped

1 medium purple onion

1 tbsp pumpkin seeds

2 tbsp olive oil

2 tbsp lemon juice

1 tsp garlic paste

1 tsp sweet chili sauce

Salt and pepper to taste

Preparation:

Add beans to a medium sieve and rinse thoroughly under cold running water. Drain and add to a bowl.

Wash the pepper and slice in half lengthwise. Remove stem and seeds. Rinse well and slice. Add to a bowl along with diced chili peppers.

Add pine nuts, sliced onions, macadamia nuts, and pumpkin seeds. Toss well to combine and set aside.

In a small bowl, whisk together olive oil, lemon juice, garlic paste, sweet chili sauce, some salt and pepper. Drizzle over salad and mix well.

Serve.

Nutrition information per serving: Kcal: 397, Protein: 16.5g, Carbs: 47.2g, Fats: 17.6g

27. Chickpea Cucumber Salad

Ingredients:

1 cup chickpeas, drained

1 jalapeno pepper, diced

1 tomato, chopped

1 cucumber, sliced

1 red bell pepper, sliced

1 onion, sliced

2 tbsp olive oil

2 tbsp lime juice

1 tbsp brown sugar

1 tsp garlic paste

¼ tsp cumin powder

Preparation:

Add chickpeas to a large sieve and rinse thoroughly under cold running water. Drain and add to a bowl along with chopped tomato, cucumber, bell pepper, and onion. Toss to combine and set aside.

Now, prepare the dressing. In a small bowl, combine together olive oil, lime juice, brown sugar, garlic paste, and cumin powder. Mix well and optionally add one teaspoon of sesame seeds.

Drizzle over the vegetable mixture and refrigerate for about 30 minutes before serving.

Optionally, sprinkle with some more lemon juice before serving.

Nutrition information per serving: Kcal: 384, Protein: 14.7g, Carbs: 54.9g, Fats: 13.7g

28. Eggplant Salad with Nuts

Ingredients:

1 medium eggplant, sliced

1 cup cherry tomatoes, sliced

½ cup corn, drained

1 medium purple onion, diced

½ red bell pepper, sliced

1 small cucumber, sliced

¼ cup almonds, toasted

2 tbsp walnuts, minced

2 tbsp pine nuts

2 tbsp lemon juice

2 tbsp vegetable oil

1 tsp Worcestershire sauce

Salt and pepper to taste

Preparation:

Preheat the oven to 400 degrees F. Line a baking sheet with

parchment paper and set aside.

Peel and slice eggplant. Arrange eggplant slices over the prepared baking sheet and sprinkle with salt. Bake for 20 minutes.

When done, remove from the oven and cool for a while. Transfer baked eggplant to serving plate and set aside.

Wash and prepare vegetables. Add to the plate along with nuts.

In a small bowl, mix together lemon juice, vegetable oil, Worcestershire sauce, salt, and pepper. Sprinkle over salad and serve.

Nutrition information per serving: Kcal: 462, Protein: 11.9g, Carbs: 42.3g, Fats: 31.5g

29. Creamy Beet Salad

Ingredients:

2 medium beets, sliced

2 eggs, boiled

1 cup plain Greek yogurt

½ cup sour cream

1 tbsp Dijon mustard

¼ cup parsley, finely chopped

3 garlic cloves, crushed

2 tbsp walnuts, finely chopped

2 tbsp almonds, finely chopped

1 cup arugula

1 tbsp grapeseed oil

Salt and pepper to taste

Preparation:

Add sliced beets to a deep pot and pour in enough water to cover. Generously sprinkle with salt and bring to a boil. Cook until fork-tender.

Remove beets from the heat and drain. Cool completely and then transfer to serving bowl.

Meanwhile, add eggs to a pot of boiling water and cook for 12 minutes. Remove from the heat and drain. Cool for a while and peel. Slice eggs and add to a bowl with beets. Set aside.

In a medium bowl, mix together Greek yogurt, sour cream, dijon, parsley, and crushed garlic. Add walnuts and almonds. Mix well again and pour over beets and eggs.

Add arugula and sprinkle with oil, salt, and pepper. Toss to combine and serve.

Nutrition information per serving: Kcal: 470, Protein: 24.8g, Carbs: 22.1g, Fats: 32.9g

30. Caesar Salad with Cashews

Ingredients:

7oz chicken breast, boneless and skinless

½ cup croutons

1 cup lettuce, chopped

1 cup baby spinach, chopped

½ cucumber, sliced

2 eggs, boiled

½ tomato, sliced

2 tbsp plain Greek yogurt

2 tbsp sour cream

2oz cashews, chopped

1 tbsp lemon juice

Salt and pepper to taste

Preparation:

Preheat the oven to 400 degrees F. Line a baking pan with parchment paper and set aside.

Add eggs to a pot of boiling water and cook for 10 minutes. Remove from the heat and drain. Cool for a while and then peel. Set aside.

Rinse the meat thoroughly under cold running water and pat dry with a kitchen towel. Place on a large cutting board and cut into bite-sized pieces. Sprinkle with salt and pepper and add to the prepared baking pan. Bake for 20-25 minutes, or until golden brown.

Remove the meat from the oven and set aside.

Meanwhile, wash and prepare vegetables. Add to a bowl along with chilled meat, sliced eggs, and cashews.

Finally, combine Greek yogurt with sour cream, lemon juice, salt, and pepper. Pour the mixture over salad and serve.

Nutrition information per serving: Kcal: 429, Protein: 34.3g, Carbs: 21.6g, Fats: 23.5g

31. Lentil Salad

Ingredients:

1 cup cooked lentils

1 medium-sized red bell pepper

½ cup sweet corn

A handful of purple cabbage, shredded

A handful of lettuce, shredded

½ tsp salt

¼ tsp black pepper, freshly ground

2 tbsp olive oil

1 tbsp sesame seeds

Preparation:

First you have to cook your lentils. Use 3 cups of water for 1 cup of dry lentils. Cooked lentils will double in size. Keep this in mind when cooking. Bring the water to a boiling point, reduce the heat to medium and cover. Cook for about 15-20 minutes. Remove from the heat and drain. Transfer to a bowl.

Wash the pepper and cut lengthwise in half. Remove the

seeds and stem. Chop into bite-sized pieces and set aside.

Combine cabbage and lettuce in a large colander. Rinse under running water and drain. Shred and set aside.

Now add other ingredients, season with salt, pepper, olive oil, and sprinkle with sesame seeds. Toss well to combine.

Nutrition information per serving: Kcal: 311, Protein: 11.6g, Carbs: 32.3g, Fats: 17.2g

32. Garlic Tuna with Asparagus and Avocado

Ingredients:

8oz fresh, wild asparagus

½ avocado, sliced

10oz tuna steak

2 garlic cloves

2 tbsp cooking oil

2 tbsp olive oil

Salt and freshly ground black pepper

¼ cup olives, sliced

Preparation:

Preheat the oil in a medium pan over medium heat. Season the tuna steak with some salt and pepper. Cook for 3-4 minutes on each side.

Remove from the pan and cool for a while. Flake the tuna steak into small pieces.

Clean and cut the asparagus into 2 inch long strips. Heat the remaining olive oil over a medium-high heat. Add asparagus and stir-fry for several minutes. Stir in garlic and mix well. Remove from the heat and use some kitchen paper to soak the excess oil.

Transfer to a serving platter and top with tuna. Add avocado and olives. Sprinkle with salt and pepper.

Serve.

Nutrition information per serving: Kcal: 385, Protein: 6.9g, Carbs: 9.7g, Fats: 37.7g

33. Crispy Beans with Lime Dressing

Ingredients:

½ red onion, sliced

1 cup green beans, cooked

3 cherry tomatoes, halved

½ red bell pepper, sliced

¼ cup of fresh lime juice

3 tbsp of olive oil

1 tsp of honey

½ small shallot, minced

1 garlic clove, crushed

¼ tsp of salt

Preparation:

In a small bowl, combine together olive oil and lime juice. Add honey, shallot, garlic, and salt. Whisk together until fully incorporated. Set aside.

Add the remaining ingredients in a serving bowl and drizzle with the prepared dressing. Toss well to combine and refrigerate for at least 30 minutes before serving.

Nutrition information per serving: Kcal: 265, Protein: 3.4g, Carbs: 19.7g, Fats: 21.6g

34. Chicken and Tofu Salad

Ingredients:

7oz chicken breast, boneless and skinless

¼ cup smoked tofu, sliced

1 cup lamb's lettuce

1 cup cherry tomatoes

½ cup button mushrooms, sliced

1 small zucchini, sliced

Salt and pepper to taste

2 tbsp olive oil

Preparation:

Wash and pat dry the meat with some kitchen paper. Cut into bite size pieces. Peel and chop zucchini.

Grease a large, non-stick grill pan with oil and heat over medium-high heat. Add the meat and cook for 7-10 minutes, stirring constantly. Remove the meat from the pan and add zucchini and mushrooms.

Continue to cook for another 10 minutes.

When done, remove from the heat and transfer to serving bowl. Add lamb's lettuce, tofu, and cherry toamtoes.

Sprinkle with olive oil, salt, and pepper. Toss well to combine and serve.

Nutrition information per serving: Kcal: 277, Protein: 24.5g, Carbs: 6.2g, Fats: 17.7g

35. Lettuce Salad with Walnuts

Ingredients:

2 cups lettuce, chopped

1 large orange, peeled

¼ cup walnuts

¼ cup dates, finely chopped

1 tbsp fresh lemon juice

Preparation:

Rinse the lettuce under cold running water and drain in a large colander. Gently squeeze with your hands and chop. Transfer to a serving bowl.

Add orange, walnuts, and dates. Sprinkle with lemon juice and toss well to combine.

Optionally, add a pinch of ground cumin and serve.

Nutrition information per serving: Kcal: 424, Protein: 11g, Carbs: 61.7g, Fats: 19.2g

36. Wild Salmon Salad with Lettuce and Fresh Lime

Ingredients:

10oz wild salmon fillets, skinless

7oz lettuce, torn

1 medium cucumber, sliced

2 eggs, boiled

½ cup sour cream

1 tbsp Dijon mustard

1 tbsp extra virgin olive oil

2 tbsp fresh lime juice

½ tsp salt

Preparation:

Preheat the oven to 425 degrees. Line a baking sheet with parchment paper and set aside.

Rinse the fillet and pat dry with a kitchen towel. Add to a cutting board and slice into 1-inch thick slices. Rub each with salt and transfer to the prepared baking sheet.

Bake for 15 minutes.

When done, remove from the oven and cool to a room temperature. Set aside.

Meanwhile, wash and prepare the vegetables. Add to serving bowl and mix well.

Add eggs to a pot of boiling water and cook for 10 minutes. When done, remove from the heat and drain the water. Cool completely and then peel. Slice eggs and add to a bowl with vegetables. Set aside.

Finally, in a small bowl, whisk together sour cream, Dijon mustard, olive oil, lime juice, and salt. Brush the salmon with this mixture and serve over vegetables and eggs.

Nutrition information per serving: Kcal: 412, Protein: 39.1g, Carbs: 11.7g, Fats: 25.3g

37. Leek Salad with Avocado and Salmon

Ingredients:

2 leeks, chopped into bite-sized pieces

7oz salmon fillet, skinless

½ avocado, sliced

1 tsp dried thyme

½ tsp dried rosemary

2 tbsp olive oil

Salt and freshly ground black pepper

Preparation:

Grease a medium skillet with olive oil and heat over high heat. Clean and wash leeks. Cut into bite-sized pieces and add to the skillet. Cook for 8-10 minutes, stirring constantly.

When done, remove leeks from the skillet and transfer to serving bowl.

Now, rub the salmon fillet with salt and pepper and add to the pan. Cook for 5-6 minutes on each side.

When done, remove from the heat and add to serving bowl

along with sliced avocado. Sprinkle with some more salt and pepper, dried thyme, and rosemary.

Toss well to combine and serve.

Nutrition information per serving: Kcal: 410, Protein: 21.6g, Carbs: 17.4g, Fats: 30.3g

38. Fresh Vegetables with Cubed Tofu

Ingredients:

8oz smoked tofu, cubed

1 large tomato, sliced

1 cup baby spinach, chopped

1 small onion, diced

1 small carrot, diced

1 green chili, diced

1 tbsp butter

1 tsp soy sauce

2 tsp oyster sauce

½ tsp garlic powder

Salt and pepper to taste

Preparation:

Melt the butter in a small pan over medium heat. Add cubed tofu and sprinkle with salt and pepper. Cook for 2-3 minutes and then add soy sauce, oyster sauce, and garlic powder. Continue to cook for another 2 minutes. Remove from the heat and transfer to a bowl.

Meanwhile, wash and prepare vegetables. Add to a bowl and mix well to combine. Optionally, season with some more salt or pepper to taste and sprinkle with some freshly squeezed lemon juice.

Serve.

Nutrition information per serving: Kcal: 309, Protein: 23.5g, Carbs: 14.4g, Fats: 18.2g

39. Spicy Avocado Salad

Ingredients

1 ripe avocado, sliced

2 red chili peppers, diced

2 cups baby spinach

1 cup arugula, chopped

1 onion, diced

2 tbsp sesame oil

1 tsp sriracha

1 tbsp soy sauce

1 tsp mirin

½ tsp garlic powder

Preparation:

Preheat a large wok pan over high heat. Sprinkle with pan with sesame oil and add sliced avocado. Cook for 2 minutes on high heat and then sprinkle with soy sauce, sriracha, mirin, and garlic powder. Continue to cook for another 2-3 minutes, stirring constantly.

Remove from the heat and transfer to bowl. Set aside.

Now, rinse and prepare the vegetables. Add to serving bowl and mix with avocado. Optionally, season with some salt or sprinkle with lime juice.

Serve.

Nutrition information per serving: Kcal: 371, Protein: 4.3g, Carbs: 18.4g, Fats: 33.5g

40. Zesty Quinoa Salad

Ingredients:

1 cup quinoa, dry

1 medium carrot, grated

1 cup green peas, drained

2 tbsp lemon juice

1 tbsp orange juice

Zest of one lemon

½ tsp garlic powder

2 tbsp olive oil

Preparation:

Add quinoa to a heavy-bottomed pot and pour in two cups of water. Sprinkle with some salt and garlic powder. Bring to a boil and reduce the heat to low. Stir well and cook until all the liquid has evaporated. Remove from the heat and transfer to a bowl.

Add grated carrot and green peas. Stir in lemon juice, orange juice, and lemon zest. Sprinkle salad with olive oil and toss to combine.

Serve immediately.

Nutrition information per serving: Kcal: 342, Protein: 11g, Carbs: 46.4g, Fats: 13g

41. Black Bean Salad with Cheese and Mushrooms

Ingredients:

1 cup black beans, drained

½ cup green peas

2 spring onions, chopped

1 cup sliced shiitake mushrooms

¼ cup cottage cheese

½ cup plain Greek yogurt

2 boiled eggs, sliced

1 tbsp olive oil

Salt and pepper to taste

Preparation:

Grease a non-stick fryin pan with olive oil and heat over medium-high heat. Add spring onions and sprinkle with salt. Cook for 3-4 minutes, stirring constantly.

Now, add shiitake mushrooms and season with some more salt and pepper. Continue to cook for 7-8 minutes, stirring constantly. Remove from the heat and set aside.

Meanwhile, boil eggs for 10 minutes. Remove from the heat and drain. Cool for a while and peeel. Transfer to a owl along with drained black beans and green peas. Add the shiiteke mixture and stir in cottage cheese. Mix all well.

Pour the Greek yogurt over salad and sprinkle with olive oil, salt, and pepper. Serve.

Nutrition information per serving: Kcal: 397, Protein: 24.6g, Carbs: 55g, Fats: 9.6g

42. Herring and Romaine Lettuce Salad

Ingredients:

7oz herring fillets, canned

1 cucumber, sliced

1 carrot, finely chopped

3 olives

1 cup romaine lettuce, torn

2 tbsp olive oil

2 tbsp lemon juice

1 tbsp dill, finely chopped

Salt and pepper to taste

½ tsp chili powder

Preparation:

Peel and thinly slice cucumber. Set aside.

Using a colander, rinse the lettuce under running water. Drain and set aside.

Now, combine cucumber, carrto and lettuce on a serving plate.

Drain herring fillets and add to serving plate. Sprinkle with salt, pepper, dill, chili powder, and olive oil. Mix well to combine and top with olives.

Refrigerate for 30 minutes before serving.

Nutrition information per serving: Kcal: 375, Protein: 24.7g, Carbs: 10.9g, Fats: 26.6g

43. Chicken Cucumber Salad

Ingredients:

7oz chicken breast, boneless and skinless

1 cucumber, sliced

1 red pepper, sliced

2 slices bread, lightly toasted

1 tomato, chopped

1 cup lettuce, chopped

2 tsp taco seasoning

2 tbsp honey

2 tbsp olive oil

2 tbsp lemon juice

½ tsp dried celery

Salt and pepper to taste

Preparation:

Preheat the oven to 350 degrees. Line a baking sheet with parchment paper and set aside.

Rinse the meat and pat dry with a kitchen towel. Cut into bite-sized pieces and add to the prepared baking sheet. Sprinkle with salt and bake for 30 minutes.

When done, remove from the oven and transfer to a bowl along with cucumber, red pepper, bread, tomato, and lettuce. Mix well and set aside.

In a small bowl, whisk together raco seasoning, honey, olive oil, lemon juice, celery, salt, and pepper. Drizzle over salad and toss to combine.

Serve.

Nutrition information per serving: Kcal: 381, Protein: 23.9g, Carbs: 35.2g, Fats: 17.3g

44. Lemon Shrimp Salad

Ingredients:

7oz cleaned shrimps

1 cup lettuce mix

½ sliced purple onion

1 chopped tomato

1 sliced carrot

½ cup chopped arugula

1 tbsp olive oil

1 tbsp lemon juice

1 tsp lemon zest

½ tsp salt

¼ tsp dried thyme

¼ tsp fresh rosemary

¼ cup white wine

Preparation:

Rinse shrimps under cold running water and drain in a large

sieve. Grease a non-stick skillet with olive oil and heat up over medium-high heat. Add shrimps and season with salt, dried thyme, and rosemary. Briefly cook for 3-4 minutes, stirring constantly.

Now, pour in the wine and give it a good stir. Continue to cook for 5 minutes.

Remove from the heat and set aside. In a large bowl, combine together lettuce, sliced onion, tomato, carrot, and arugula. Add shrimps and sprinkle with lemon juice and lemon zest. If necessary, season with some more salt or dried herbs.

Serve immediately.

Nutritional information per serving: Kcal: 483, Protein: 48.6g, Carbs: 22g, Fats: 18g

45. Thai Salmon Salad

Ingredients:

4oz thinly sliced salmon fillets

¼ cup sliced cucumber

2 tbsp fresh lime juice

1 tbsp sweet chili sauce

1 tsp brown sugar

1 sliced red chili pepper

1 tsp chopped Thai basil

1 1-inch grated ginger knob

2 tsp finely chopped peanuts

a few lettuce leaves for serving

Preparation:

In a small bowl, combine lime juice, sweet chili sauce, peanuts, and sugar. Stir to combine and then add salmon fillets. Mix to coat well and let it marinate for 20 minutes.

Meanwhile, prepare the salad. Combine cucumber, chili pepper, basil, and basil on a sheet of lettuce leaves.

Use half of the previously prepared marinade and drizzle over the salad.

Now, preheat the avocado oil in a small saucepan over a medium-high heat. Add salmon and cook for 2-3 minutes on each side. Top the salad with salmon and drizzle with the remaining marinade.

Sprinkle all with fresh ginger and serve immediately.

Nutritional information per serving: Kcal: 456, Protein: 35.7g, Carbs: 16g, Fats: 29.1g

46. Cold Chicken and Broccoli Salad with Rice

Ingredients:

3oz chicken breast

1 cup chopped broccoli

1 sliced red bell pepper

¼ cup rice

2 tbsp soy sauce

2 tsp sesame oil

1 tbsp rice vinegar

½ tsp chili powder

1 tsp sugar

¼ tsp white pepper

Salt to taste

Preparation:

Rinse the chicken under cold running water and pat dry with some kitchen paper. Place on a large cutting board and cut into bite-sized pieces. Set aside.

Grease a large wok pan with sesame oil and heat up over

high heat. Add chopped chicken and cook for 4-5 minutes, stirring constantly. Now add bell pepper and broccoli. Drizzle with soy sauce and rice vinegar and sprinkle with chili powder, sugar, salt, and freshly ground white pepper.

Continue to cook until broccoli has completely softened.

Remove from the heat and set aside.

Prepare the rice according to package instructions or place in a small saucepan and pour in 3/4 cup of water. Sprinkle with some salt and bring it to a boil. Reduce the heat to low and cook until all the liquid has evaporated.

Serve with the chicken mixture.

Nutritional information per serving: Kcal: 457, Protein: 27.3g, Carbs: 58g, Fats: 12.1g

47. Baked Chicken Salad

Ingredients:

10oz chicken breast

1 cup arugula

1 cup cherry tomatoes

1 cup baby spinach

2 tsp olive oil

1 tbsp lemon juice

½ tsp chili powder

1 tbsp soy sauce

Salt and pepper to taste

Preparation:

Preheat the oven to 350 degrees F. Line a baking sheet with some parchment paper and set aside.

In a small bowl, whisk together olive oil, soy sauce, lemon juice, chili powder, and soy sauce. Season with salt and pepper to taste and set aside.

Rinse well the meat and generously brush with the

prepared mixture. Bake for 25-30 minutes.

When done, remove from the oven and cool for a while. Transfer to a cutting board and cut into approximately 1/4-inch thick slices. Place in a bowl along with the remaining ingredients and optionally season with some more salt or sprinkle with lemon juice.

Toss to combine and serve.

Nutritional information per serving: Kcal: 464, Protein: 64.4g, Carbs: 11g, Fats: 17g

48. Shrip Taco Cole Slaw Salad

Ingredients:

2 taco shells

3oz peeled and deveined shrimps

2 sliced cherry tomatoes

1 cup shredded cabbage

½ grated carrot

2 tbsp sour cream

2 tbsp Greek yogurt

2 tsp white vinegar

1 tsp dry mustard

1 tsp dried celery

salt and pepper to taste

lemon juice to taste

Preparation:

Prepare taco shells according to package directions and set aside.

In a large bowl, combine together cabbage and carrot. Add sour cream, Greek yogurt, mustard, vinegar, celery, salt and pepper to taste. Toss well to combine and set aside.

Preheat a non-stick grill pan or an electric grill to high heat. Grill shrimps for 3-4 minutes. Stuff each taco shell with the cabbage mixture, add tomatoes, and top with grilled shrimps.

Drizzle with freshly squeezed lime juice and serve immediately.

Nutritional information per serving: Kcal: 448, Protein: 28.2g, Carbs: 45g, Fats: 18.3g

49. Quinoa with Salmon and Beans

Ingredients:

¼ cup quinoa

¼ cup black beans

3oz salmon fillet

1 chopped tomato

2 tbsp drained corn

1 tsp ground dried shiitake

½ tsp salt

¼ tsp dried thyme

1 tbsp lemon juice

1 tbsp finely chopped parsley

Preparation:

Place quinoa in a small saucepan and pour in 1/2 cup of water. Sprinkle with some salt and bring to a boil. Reduce the heat to medium-low and simmer until all the liquid has evaporated. Stir occasionally.

Remove from the heat and set aside.

Grease a non-stick frying pan with some cooking spray and heat up over medium-high heat. Rinse fillets under cold running water and place on a cutting board. Using a sharp knife, cut into bite-sized pieces and transfer to the frying pan.

Cook for 3-4 minutes, stirring constantly. Stir in chopped tomato and pour in about 1/4 cup of water. Continue to cook for 5 minutes.

Finally, stir in cooked quinoa, corn, and black beans. Season with salt, thyme, and ground shiitake. Stir all well and remove from the heat.

Sprinkle with fresh parsley and lemon juice before serving.

Nutritional information per serving: Kcal: 464, Protein: 34.7g, Carbs: 63g, Fats: 9.7g

50. Creamy Chicken Salad with Cheese

Ingredients:

7oz chicken breast

1 cup cherry tomatoes

1 cup arugula

1 cup lettuce

½ sliced purple onion

2 tbsp feta cheese

½ tsp dried chives

¼ tsp dried oregano

½ tsp salt

1 tbsp lemon juice

1 tbsp olive oil

Preparation:

Preheat a non-stick grill pan or an electric grill to high heat.

Rinse the meat under cold running water and rub with salt, chives, and oregano. Grill for 4-5 minutes on each side and remove from the heat.

Transfer to a bowl and add vegetables. Sprinkle with olive oil, lemon juice and top with cheese.

Serve immediately.

Nutritional information per serving: Kcal: 468, Protein: 48g, Carbs: 16.8g, Fats: 24g

51. Shrimp Salad with Avocado

Ingredients:

1 cup peeled and deveined shrimps

1 chopped onion

¼ sliced avocado

1 cup arugula

1 cup cherry tomatoes

¼ sliced mango

1 tbsp sweet chili sauce

¼ tsp salt

¼ tsp garlic powder

2 tsp olive oil

Preparation:

Grease a small skillet with olive oil and heat up over medium heat. Add onions and cook until translucent.

Now, add shrimps and season with some salt. Continue to cook for 5 more minutes.

Stir in chili sauce and sprinkle with some more salt and

garlic powder. Remove from the heat and transfer to a bowl.

Add the remaining ingredients and mix all well. Serve immediately.

Nutritional information per serving: Kcal: 445, Protein: 24.3g, Carbs: 42.3g, Fats: 21.8g

52. Buckwheat Salad with Avocado and Mushrooms

Ingredients:

5oz chicken breast

¼ chopped avocado

1 cup sliced button mushrooms

¼ cup buckwheat groats

½ grated carrot

1 diced chili pepper

1 tsp olive oil

1 tbsp fresh dill

½ tsp garlic powder

salt and pepper to taste

Preparation:

In a small saucepan combine buckwheat with 1/2 cup of water. Season with salt and cook over medium heat for 8-10 minutes, stirring occasionally.

Remove from the heat and set aside. Rinse the meat and cut into bite-sized pieces. Place in a bowl and sprinkle with olive oil, salt, pepper, and garlic powder. Mix all well and set aside.

Preheat a non-stick frying pan over medium-high heat and add the chicken. Cook for 3-4 minutes, stirring constantly.

Now, add mushrooms, diced chili, and avocado. Give it a good stir and continue to cook for another 3-4 minutes. Stir in groats and season to taste.

Sprinkle with freshly grated carrot and finely chopped dill.

Nutritional information per serving: Kcal: 450, Protein: 33.1g, Carbs: 42.6g, Fats: 18g

ADDITIONAL TITLES FROM THIS AUTHOR

70 Effective Meal Recipes to Prevent and Solve Being Overweight: Burn Fat Fast by Using Proper Dieting and Smart Nutrition

By Joe Correa CSN

48 Acne Solving Meal Recipes: The Fast and Natural Path to Fixing Your Acne Problems in Less Than 10 Days!

By Joe Correa CSN

41 Alzheimer's Preventing Meal Recipes: Reduce or Eliminate Your Alzheimer's Condition in 30 Days or Less!

By Joe Correa CSN

70 Effective Breast Cancer Meal Recipes: Prevent and Fight Breast Cancer with Smart Nutrition and Powerful Foods

By Joe Correa CSN

www.ingramcontent.com/pod-product-compliance
Lightning Source LLC
Chambersburg PA
CBHW052027070526
44584CB00016B/1942